EGYPTIAN ART

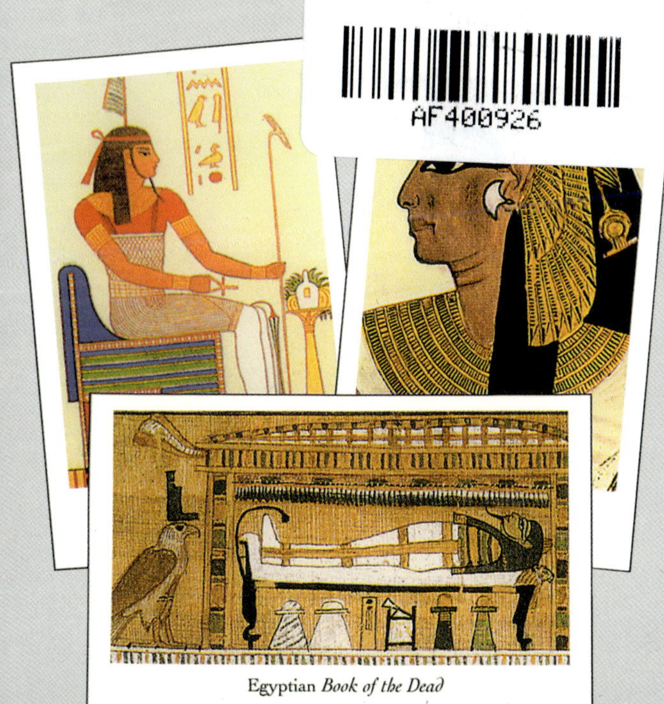

Egyptian *Book of the Dead*

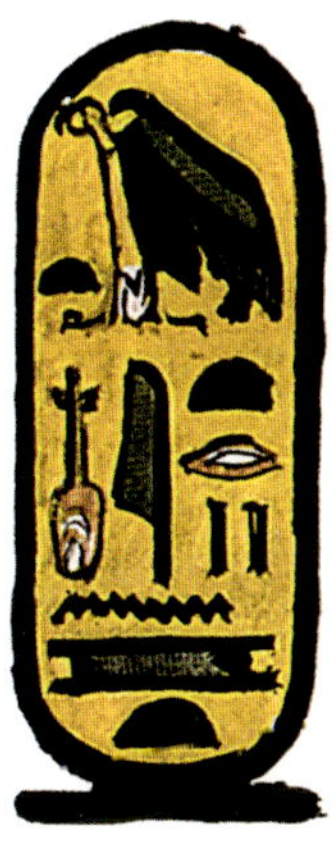

Hieroglyphs from the Tomb of
Nefertari. Thebes.

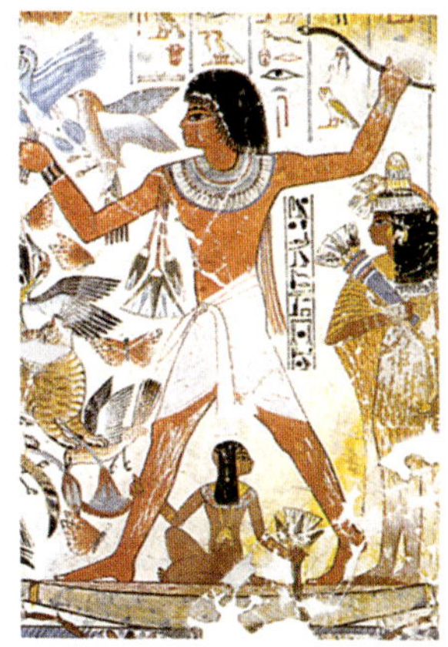

Tomb of Nebamun. Thebes.

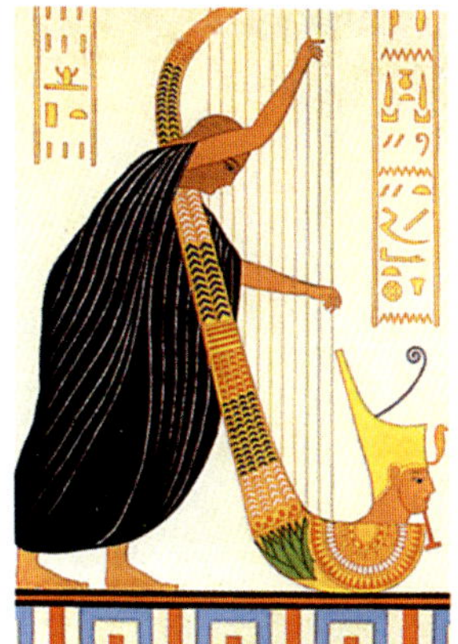

Tomb of Ramses III.
Valley of the Kings, Thebes.

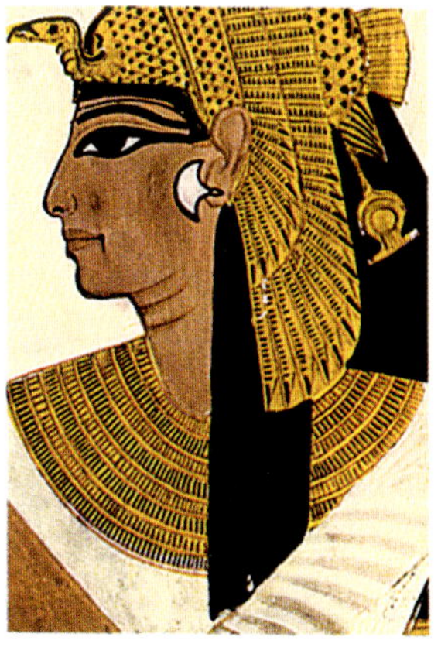

Tomb of Nefertari.
Valley of the Queens, Thebes.

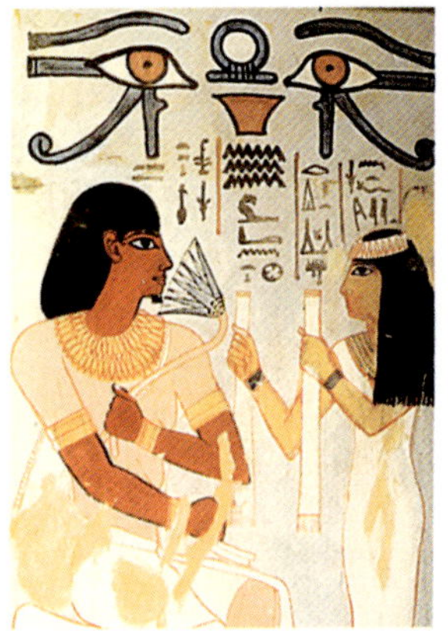

Tomb of Sennufer.
Sheikh Abd el-Qurna, Thebes.

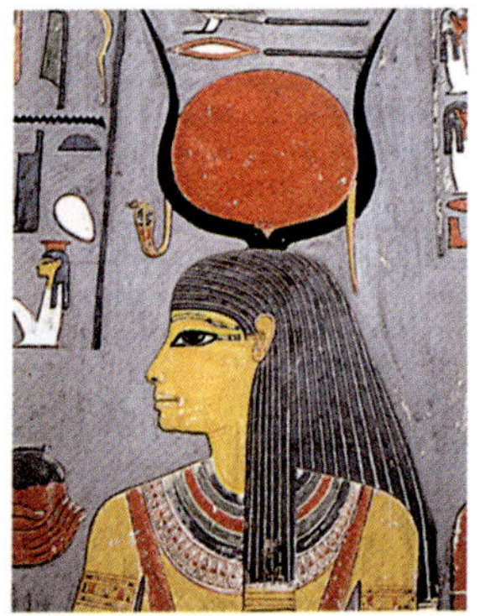

The Goddess Isis,
Tomb of Haremhab.
Valley of the Kings, Thebes.

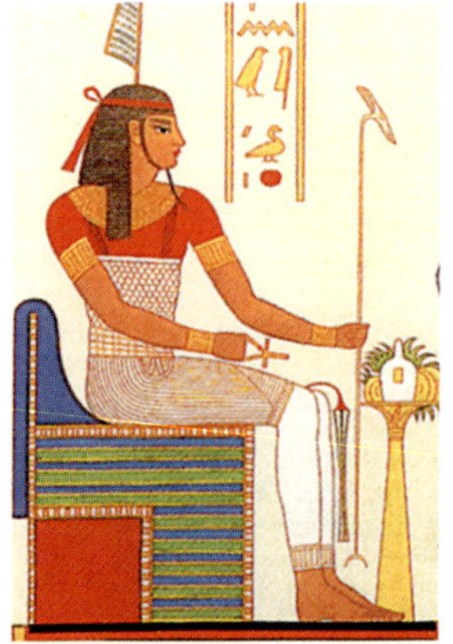

Tomb of Ramses III.
Valley of the Kings, Thebes.

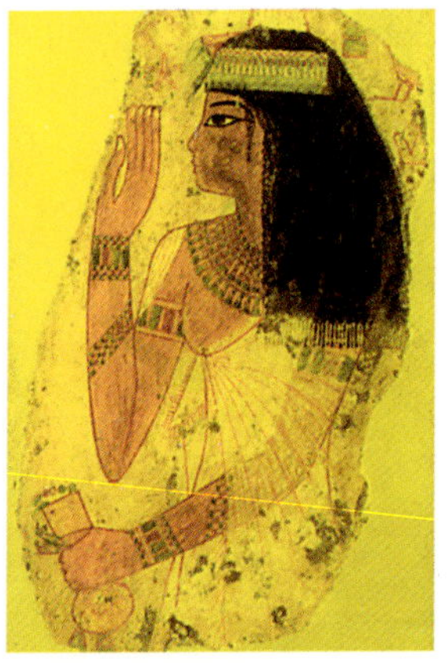

Painting of the woman Tjepu.
Thebes.

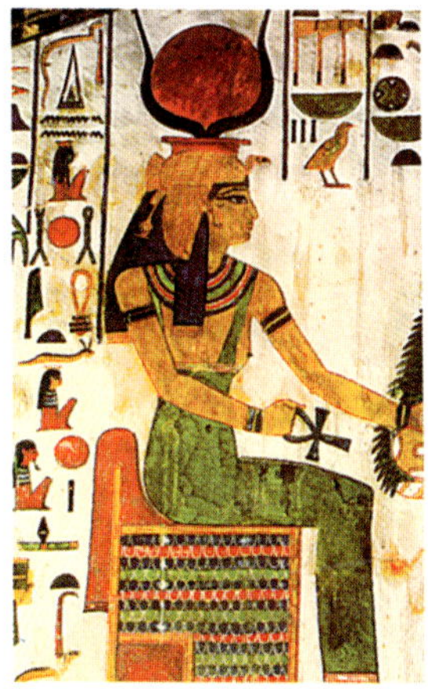

Tomb of Nofretari. Thebes.

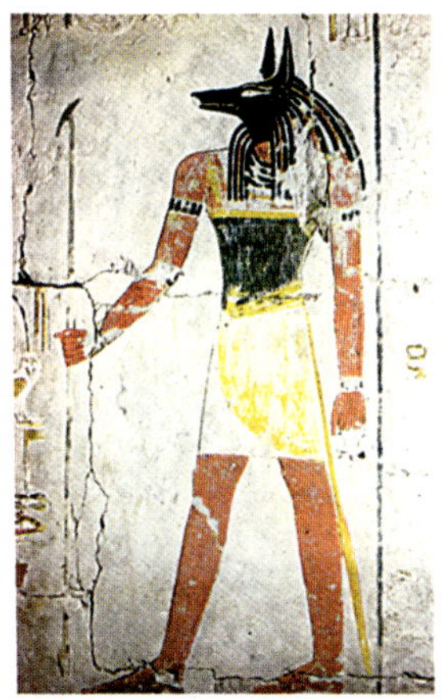

Temple of Hatshepsut. Deir el Bahari.

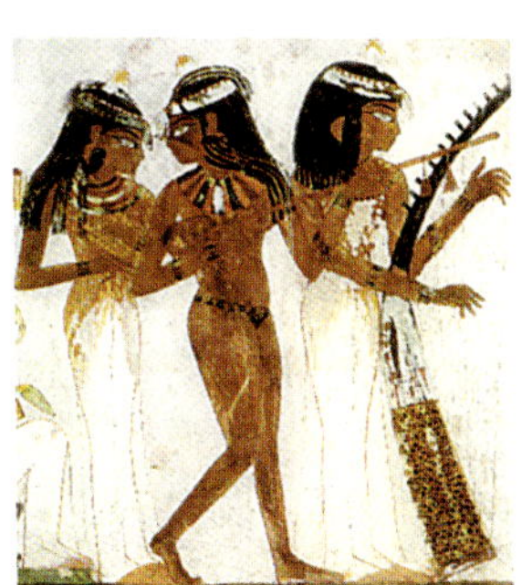

Women Musicians,
Tomb of Nakht. Thebes.

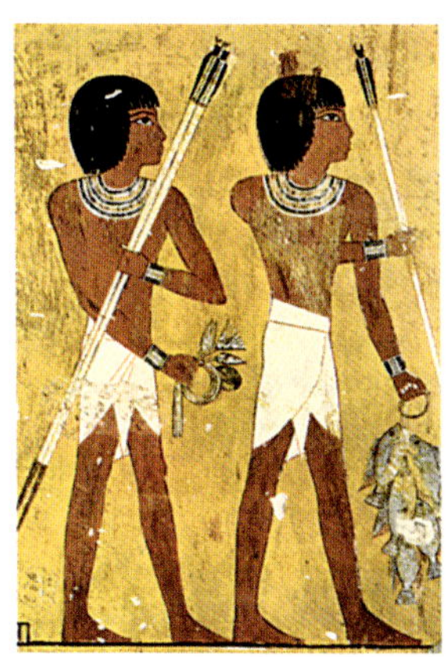

Tomb of Kenamun. Thebes.

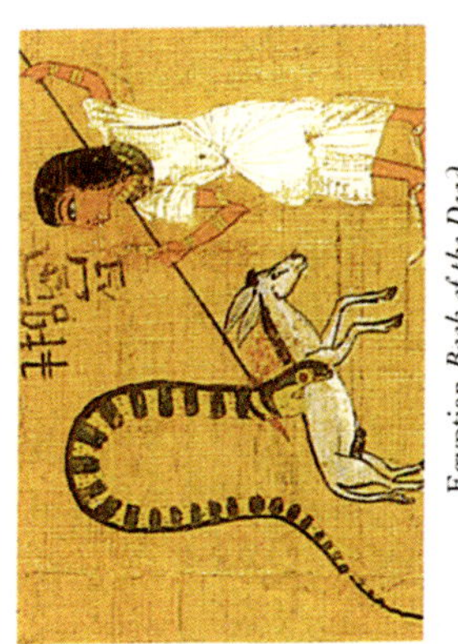

Egyptian Book of the Dead

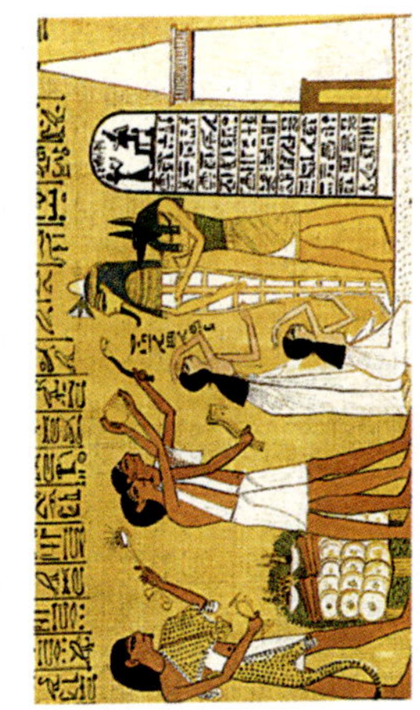

Egyptian Book of the Dead

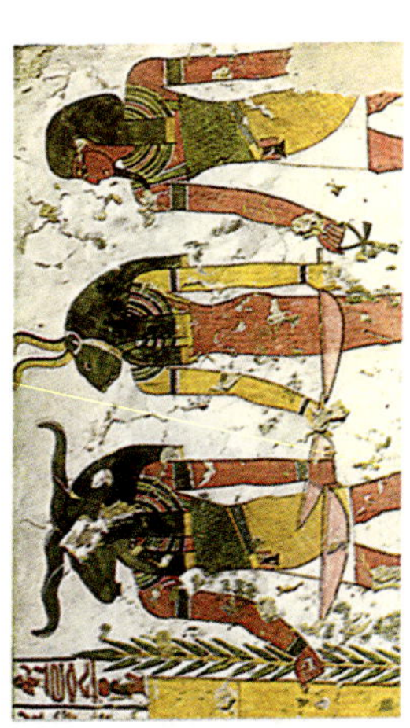

Tomb of Nofretari. Thebes.

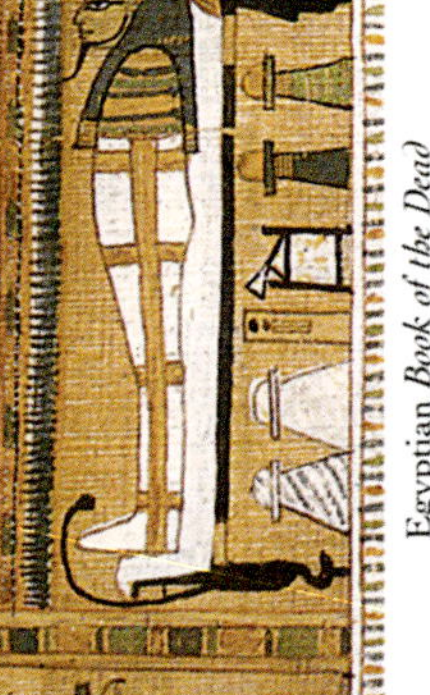

Egyptian Book of the Dead

Egyptian Art: 16 Art Stickers is a new work,
first published by Dover Publications in 2000.

ISBN-13: 978-0-486-41354-9
ISBN-10: 0-486-41354-3

Manufactured in the United States by Phoenix Color
41354311   2024
www.doverpublications.com

These 16 stickers reproduce centuries-old art from the tombs and temples of ancient Egypt. Add these exquisite gods, goddesses, hieroglyphs, and other ancient images to gifts, stationery, laptops, and more.

Edited by Anna Samuel

Not intended for children under 4

Acid-free inks, paper and adhesives

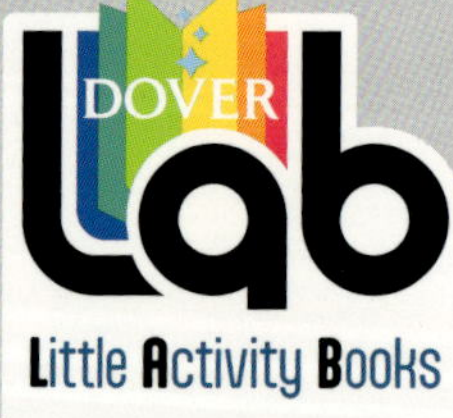

www.doverpublications.com

$2.50 USA

PRINTED IN THE USA

ISBN 978-0-486-41354-9

ART/INDIVIDUAL ARTISTS